# The Bartender's Guide to Financial Freedom

or

# How to Quit Being Broke

Tony X. Lee

Leah Ward-Lee

Copyright © 2018 Tony X. Lee & Leah Ward-Lee

No part of this book may be reproduced or transmitted in any form or by any means without written permission of the author.

All rights reserved.

Published by: LWL Enterprises, Inc.
P.O. Box 702862
4475 Trinity Mills Road
Dallas, TX 75370-2862

ISBN: 1-945484-05-5
ISBN-13: 978-1-945484-05-6

## NOTE FROM THE AUTHOR

We've all been there: you finished your shift and cleaned and closed the bar, got home and fed the dog, finally took those wet socks off, and counted your money. Then you thought about what you made yesterday, and the day before that, and the day before that.

You pour a glass or pop a beer and sit down… and a thought pops into your head, "Wait a sec, how am I working all these hours and coming home with money every day, but I'm still damn-near broke?"

Coming from someone who started working in a restaurant at 15, was bartending at 19, and spent the next 15 years as a bartender or manager, I know that thought well. I remember 114-hour workweeks with thousands in my wallet, only to be broke two weeks later.

That's what I and my co-author, Leah Ward-Lee, are going to address in this book. I did it for too long and have known and loved too many fantastic bartenders and servers who worked their asses off and still struggled to pay the bills.

So, read on, get out the budget and the workbook, and we'll help you get that financial freedom.

Put a tenth of the effort into this that you do every shift slingin' drinks, being a therapist and babysitter, pleasing your bosses, and it'll pay off.

The juice is worth the squeeze.

- Tony X. Lee

Tony X. Lee & Leah Ward-Lee

Contents

Step 1: Make the Decision ................................................................. 1
Step 2: Analyze Your Monthly Commitment .......................................... 5
Step 3: Track Your Progress Daily ....................................................... 20
Step 4: Develop Your Contingency Plan ............................................... 25
Step 5: Tame the Paper Tiger ............................................................. 30
Step 6: Hold a Weekly Business Meeting ............................................. 36
Step 7: Raise Your Credit Score .......................................................... 41
Step 8: Build Long-Term Wealth ......................................................... 53
Step 9: Plan Your Next Chapter .......................................................... 65
Step 10: Getting Started .................................................................... 80
ACKNOWLEDGEMENTS .................................................................... 101
ABOUT THE AUTHORS ..................................................................... 102

## Step 1:  Make the Decision

I'd flown to Jacksonville, Florida, then driven over to Amelia Island to enjoy a four-day vacation with my dad.  As I stood on the beach and looked out at the ocean I felt as if I'd arrived at the place where I was supposed to be.

As I began to plan my relocation, I realized I was going to have to make some changes in the way I'd been managing my finances.  I was physically exhausted from working doubles and clopens, but more than that I was mentally exhausted from the stress associated with never having enough money to cover my monthly expenses.

It was becoming increasingly mystifying to me, after nineteen years of food and beverage service and management, that even pulling in hundreds of thousands of dollars and working so much, I was still always fighting to cover my bills.  Working 14-shift weeks and being behind a busy bar 358 days a year was wearing me out, physically and emotionally.

I could tell you too many horror stories and dumb mistakes I made because I was tired, or because I was frustrated with always being the one capable and willing to kill myself for a job. One that stands out was when I was the general manager and head bartender of a club that was located about 20 miles from my condo. I'd been handed the keys to the place after working at another club for about two weeks. The drive to work could be a half hour or could take two hours plus on the Dallas highways.

My regular schedule required me to be there every day around 11 AM and not pry myself out of there until the next morning by 5 AM so I'd miss morning rush hour on my way home. There was always so much to do between hiring and training new staff, ordering and helping to prep product and alcohol, constantly checking and re-checking the money, handling all the marketing, and the myriad set of responsibilities required to keep a club running smoothly.

I just kept taking it all on as well as being behind the bar from 2 PM to 2 AM every day. I could handle it. I was strong. And it worked for a while. In the first two months, the weekly sales increased from $12k a week to over $40k.

However, to keep myself going I was drinking half a bottle of vodka and half a bottle of whiskey a day, but I was making money hand over fist.

One day, after completing a stretch of fourteen straight days before I had a night off, then nineteen, then seventeen, I was driving back to the club, falling asleep while on the phone with my new assistant who was having trouble getting our live crawfish in and I fell asleep while reaching for a 5-hour energy drink.

I couldn't have been out long but I woke up to red brake lights a half moment before I took my F-150 right through three other vehicles. All four vehicles were completely totaled.

I could have killed someone or myself. What we're capable of when we're blind tired is astounding. I vaguely recall my best friend picking me up and cleaning the blood off me and borrowing someone's phone to call and make sure the shift at the club was covered.

I don't remember buying a new truck the next day. I don't remember going back to work the day after that or much of the next week. That was years ago but I still have the scars, both physical and emotional.

Most of the money I'd made went to replacing the truck and to insurance, but I got right back to work because that's what I'd trained myself to do.

Standing on the beautiful beach on Amelia that day, I knew I had to make a change. We can make money all day every day, but until we learn to save it and have it work for us, what's the point? The change I needed to make was the genesis for this book.

After consulting my financial guru and coming up with a plan, the hard part started. It's not easy to develop a budget, and it's even harder sticking to it, but I made the decision. No matter how difficult it was going to be, it was better than being tired all the time, dealing with the stress and worry that my lights would be cut off or that I would have to pick up more shifts just to pay for the monthly HOA expense on the condo.

We can make money all day every day, but until we learn to save it, and have it work for us, what's the point? If my story sounds familiar, I implore you, make the decision and promise yourself you'll stick with it. It will pay off and we're here to help.

Now let's get down to business.

# Step 2: Analyze Your Monthly Commitment

Now that you've made the decision, the first step is to list all your current monthly obligations. Everything you owe or have to pay on a monthly basis should be collected and totaled. For example:

| \multicolumn{5}{c}{CURRENT MONTHLY FINANCIAL COMMITMENT} |||||
|---|---|---|---|---|
| DUE DATE | CATEGORY | MONTHLY AMOUNT | TOTAL LONG TERM | COMMENTS |
| 1st | Rent | $675.00 | | |
| 1st | Savings | $273.00 | | 50% to short-term; 50% to long-term |
| 5th | Car Insurance | $162.00 | | |
| 6th | Health Insurance | $186.00 | | |
| 7th | Phone | $118.00 | | |
| 9th | Wifi/Netflix | $53.00 | | |
| 10th | Car Note | $305.00 | $14,000.00 | 50 Months Remaining |
| 17th | Kohl's | $55.00 | $600.00 | Maxed out |
| 17th | Electricity | $85.00 | | |
| 23rd | Renter's Insurance | $36.00 | | |
| 30th | Water | $35.00 | | |
| Daily | Food, Gas, Misc $25 per day | $750.00 | | |
| TOTAL | | $2,733.00 | | |
| # OF SHIFTS | | 20 | | |
| AVERAGE PER SHIFT | | $136.65 | | |

Now, let's talk about each category of expense.

**RENT:**  Every bartender should be thrilled to have this expense. It's the expense that, when paid, allows you to live independently and make your own decisions. Even when you own your own place you'll have this category. It might be in the form of a monthly homeowner's association fee and/or annual property tax or it could be the amount you put away each month for home repairs and improvements.

Although this expense is not discretionary, the amount you spend is your choice, but is largely dictated by the cost of living in your zip code and whether you live alone or with others who share the expense.

**SAVINGS:**  This is a critical category of expense. If you don't budget for it and sock it away every month, you're one emergency away from disaster. You may be one broken finger or sick week away from your life being too expensive to afford.

These disasters can show up in many forms and by not saving you're inviting them. For example, if you don't put away money for your taxes, you can end up owing the IRS and paying a fine. If you don't get your oil changed on a regular basis your car won't last as long and you might end up with expensive repairs before you've even paid it off. If you show up late for work too many times or get into it with your boss and get fired you might not be able to pay next month's rent. Wouldn't you like the financial freedom to not work every day? If you don't save for your retirement – how will you ever put down the bar key and put your feet up?

Your savings should be split between short-term, which includes emergency funds, and long-term savings. Each has a different purpose.

Your emergency fund should be your starting point. This is the fund that's going to prevent one of the disasters I just mentioned from making you broke while allowing you to remain financially stable. It should contain two months of living expenses. This allows you to go to the dentist when you should instead of waiting until you have a cavity. It pays for an unexpected car repair, a plumber, or repairing your cell phone. When you take money out of our emergency fund because you haven't yet had enough time to fully fund it, it needs to be replaced. This is crucial.

Your short-term savings is what allows you to make wise short-term decisions and can be started just a soon as you've put enough away for your emergency fund. This is where you can start to get ahead of the game. When you start out, this is where you put the funds that you plan to spend over the next year. This pays for your contact lenses, your tune-up or new tires, your annual medical deductible, the down payment on a new car, and Christmas. I worked every

Christmas for eight years straight to be able afford to buy Christmas presents. Isn't that crazy?

When you really start to accumulate a balance in your short-term savings account you give yourself the opportunity to start living the American Dream of owning your own home or starting a business or buying into your bar and eventually having other bartenders make your money for you.

Your long-term savings is for your future. The need to save for this is more important than ever before. Not since the days when our grandparents retired could Americans expect to receive a pension that would support them in their old age.

Our parents relied on Social Security and their Individual Retirement Accounts and, if they haven't yet retired, as of this moment, depending upon their ages, even that's at risk.

If it's at risk for our parents, what's that mean for us? We all know we need to start saving now; however, more than 50% of American families have no retirement savings. What they're giving up is not only their future financial stability, but also, they're giving away free money. Who doesn't want free money?

This all sounds like "blah, blah, blah" if you're short every month just paying the bills. We'll address that in Step 3 and in Step 8 we'll address how to build long-term wealth.

**CAR INSURANCE:** The amount you pay for car insurance isn't just based on the value of your car and your driving record. If you've borrowed to buy the car, you have to pay for full coverage; this typically doubles the cost of your monthly insurance premium. The amount you pay is also based upon your credit score. (Step 7 talks about how to raise your credit score.)

**HEALTH INSURANCE:** The next category of expenses is health insurance. As of now, our current administration is working to repeal the Affordable Care Act which requires all Americans to have health insurance. Regardless of your political leanings, when our government backs up their political beliefs with laws we need to understand the financial and medical implications.

If you have no employer-sponsored health care plan and you haven't purchased health care insurance you won't have access to preventive care. This means you're rolling the dice and hoping you won't get sick and need medical care. If you do, you'll be seeking care with a "doc in the box" or, worse yet, at an emergency room. The team that treats you will assess the specific problem, treat that only, and you'll be presented with a whopping big bill. I can attest to this issue while writing this book with two broken fingers and waiting for my bar-rotted fingernails to grow back.

Trust me on this, you'll just be throwing money away. Even after two fingers on my right hand swelled up so much I couldn't bend my fingers, I had to wait three weeks for a day off. I went to two different roadside doc in the boxes and was handed nearly useless antibiotics at the cost of $325 a visit. If I had taken the time to review the health insurance that I was already paying for, I would've not only had a primary care physician, I would' have saved nearly $700. That's a losing dice roll all day every day.

If you're currently healthy and expect to remain that way, there's a way to minimize your costs and not spend a bundle for insurance you might not need. It's a three-activity process:

**Activity 1:** Find a plan that is a "qualifying high-deductible health plan." These plans come with a high deductible, but kick in and cover you in a catastrophic situation when your medical costs are significant.

**Activity 2:** Establish a Healthcare Savings Account (HSA). The magic in this is that your money accumulates and is available to you for any medical expense including dental, vision, and prescriptions. Unlike flexible spending accounts, the funds don't expire at the end of year so you don't have to guess how much you might need to cover any upcoming or unplanned expenses for next year. You typically contribute to these monthly with pre-tax dollars.

Think about that for a minute. The lowest personal tax rate for 2018 is 10%, and that goes up to 15% if you earn more than $9,525. So, at a minimum, every dollar you put into an HSA is automatically worth $1.10. Compare HSA plans to find one with the lowest maintenance fee and a plan that will process your claims easily. It's a monthly expense, but absolutely worth it.

**Activity 3:** After making certain your healthcare insurance company and your health service account company are compatible, sign up for both. No more worry about stepping on broken glass or super-gluing a cut closed so you can work. WooHoo!

**PHONE:** It's become a fact of life that we're all tethered to our phones, but that doesn't mean this is a category of expense we can't reduce over time if we also invest a little time in some activities to prevent us from needing to spend even more than our monthly plan.

**Activity 1: Prevent a Loss** Most smart phones have a "find my phone" application. The kicker is that if you lose your phone and haven't set up this app before that happens, it's too late. After having my phone stolen from an employee bathroom while taking over the main bar at a place with 106 beers on tap, I still had to pay $275 to get a new phone because I hadn't taken six minutes to set this up. Take the time to download the app and set it up now before this happens. You'll also have to set up the app on another device such as an iPad or computer so you can use that device to find the phone. Another option is to set up "Family Sharing" so that someone you designate can "see" where your phone is.

I can hear you groaning as you read this and you're thinking, "Just one more thing I don't have time to do. If only I had time to …."

We'll address time management in Step 6 when we establish a weekly business meeting, but for now either get it on your "to do" list or just stop reading for a minute and do it. If you opt to add it to your "to do" list then adopt Sharon Knight's mantra in <u>How To Get Your S\*\*T Together</u> of 'Wallet, Keys, Phone' before you walk out the door.

**Activity 2: Change Providers or Plans.** When your next statement comes look at the charges. Are you using what you're paying for? Are you paying extra charges? Is your current phone or plan eligible for an upgrade?

After reviewing this information, compare mobile plans in your area. If you find one that's less, call your current provider and find out how to lower your rates. If they don't offer that, let them know you'll call them back. Then call the lower-cost provider and determine if there are any other charges to switch.

**Activity 3: Hanging onto or Upgrading Your Cellphone.** If your account indicates that you're eligible for an upgrade, it typically means you have completed making payments on your phone and your monthly bill should have been reduced. If that didn't happen and this is the first month you've been eligible, call them and find out if it will be reduced and by how much.

Phones today are ridiculously expensive, particularly when you choose to upgrade to the next model. The companies producing phones are marketing geniuses and work hard to convince you that upgrading is essential. (You don't have the new features now and you're getting along fine, right?)

If you absolutely need to replace your phone, unlocked phones are available for hundreds of dollars less than buying the phone from a carrier or direct from the manufacturer, either new or used. eBay offers the following information on buying and setting up an unlocked cellphone:

"An unlocked phone is a cell phone or smartphone that isn't tied to any specific phone service provider." This means that the phone can be made compatible with any mobile network that allows customers to set up an account with their own unlocked smartphone or mobile devices. While most phone service providers offer this option, many will not be very helpful with the process of setting up an unlocked phone because they want to sell their own phones to customers at a markup. It is up to the consumer to figure out how to set up an unlocked phone with a phone provider that can access calling, messaging (MMS), and data services.

Fortunately, the setup process is not overly complicated. It simply requires replacing the old SIM card with a new SIM card that is linked to the service provider's network. Some service providers will be willing to sign the consumer up for a phone plan and sell the consumer a SIM card for the phone. You should be able to retain the same phone number, although you should check with your service provider. The only unlockable cell phones are those that use the Global System for Mobile communication (GSM). These phones can be purchased directly from phone manufacturers, electronics stores and websites, or online at auction sites like eBay.

**INTERNET/WIFI/TV:** The options here are endless and continue to change, and availability can be dependent upon location.

Basic Internet and WIFI can be purchased relatively inexpensively, often for less than $40 per month. It goes without saying that the costs go up as you add capability and services.

Just adding basic television services can double the cost. There are other options if you can be specific about what you want. Just type in *compare internet options in my area* and you'll get a list of the Internet Service Providers available to you. I found www.bestfreestreaming.com to be particularly informative. First, get the services you need - you can always add more later.

**CAR NOTE:** One of your goals should be to pay off your car note early. Regardless of the interest rate, if you have a car note with anything more than zero interest, you are paying more for the vehicle than it's worth.

| | Auto Loan Based on Credit Rating | | | |
|---|---|---|---|---|
| | Needs Improvement | Fair | Good | Excellent |
| Car Loan | $15,665.00 | $15,665.00 | $15,665.00 | $15,665.00 |
| Term | 60 | 60 | 60 | 60 |
| Interest Rate | 7.74% | 5.60% | 4.49% | 2.99% |
| Monthly Payment | $315.68 | $299.94 | $291.97 | $281.41 |
| Total Paid | $18,940.80 | $17,996.40 | $17,518.20 | $16,884.60 |
| Cost of Credit | $3,275.80 | $2,331.40 | $1,853.20 | $1,219.60 |
| Opportunity Cost | $2,056.20 | $1,111.80 | $633.60 | |
| Monthly Poor Credit Cost | $34.27 | $18.53 | $10.56 | |

The *Cost of Credit* line shows the premium you are paying to have a vehicle that is probably depreciating faster than you are paying for it. The amount you are paying is largely based on your credit score. (Look at the difference in the total amount paid between someone whose score falls in the *Needs Improvement* and someone in the *Excellent* column.)

When I unexpectedly totaled my truck while driving to work after working seventeen-hour days for more than two weeks straight, I was clearing $400-$1600 a week, but still had to call Mom for a loan and have her co-sign just to get a used vehicle. It seems silly to me now that I didn't have that money stacked, but I hadn't yet made the decision to be financially free and stable. This is what we want to help you avoid.

We'll begin work on raising your credit score in Step 7, but for now there are two activities you can do to get your car loan paid off more quickly. And you'll be raising your credit score while doing these.

**Activity 1:** You've probably already done this, but if not, set up an automated monthly payment that's deducted from your checking account.

**Activity 2:** Call the loan company and arrange to pay an extra $10 a month. This will take a few minutes to set up but it's worth it.

**CREDIT CARD DEBT:** Credit cards are wonderful tools to buy what you want when you want or need. Let's say that Marc Anthony shirt you *had* to buy because it was on sale is now at full price or more; if you put it on your credit card and didn't pay it off when the payment was due you're literally throwing money in the garbage. Credit card debt sucks!

I refused to get a card for three years after paying off my old debt. It's a struggle to get most things done without a card, but I managed because I was tired of paying "fees" for things I hadn't yet acquired.

If you're already in debt, there are two activities you can take:

**Activity 1:** Take any credit cards that have a balance you can't pay to zero when the bill arrives out of your wallet. Either cut them up or place them in an envelope and put them where you store the rest of your important papers. Trust that credit card companies will happily send you new cards later.

**Activity 2:** The payment you make (on time!) each month should, at a minimum, be the amount owed plus the finance charge. Otherwise the balance takes much longer to pay off. You're just giving away the money you worked hard for.

**UTILITIES:** Your water and your electricity can, to some extent, be opportunities to keep a little more of your hard-earned money in your pocket.

**Water:** If you live in an apartment that doesn't have a separate water meter you're going to pay a percent of the overall bill. If, however, you get a bill that comes in your name or you live in a house, you can typically shave 10% off the bill just by not running water frivolously, like when you're shaving or brushing your teeth.

**Electricity:** Typically the biggest portion of your electricity bill is from your heat in the winter and your air conditioning in the summer. There are several activities that can shave at least 15% off your bill every month.

- **Activity 1:** When you leave for your shift, turn your thermostat down a few degrees in the winter or up a few degrees in the summer. Jameson or Duke won't be uncomfortable while you're gone and those few degrees won't take long to recover.

- **Activity 2:** Change your furnace filter. I can't stress this enough. A clogged filter will greatly run up your costs and can even lead to water damage in your unit or the one downstairs. This only takes a couple of minutes and would've saved me from having to replace my neighbor's ceiling if I had been smart and replaced the damned thing regularly.

- **Activity 3:** Invest in a ceiling fan. In the winter set it to push the hot air back down and in the summer set it to pull the cool air up from the floor.

**RENTER'S INSURANCE:** This is typically required if you're renting. (If you've bought your place, this is homeowner's insurance.) The basic cost of this insurance is based on the value of the property being insured and your credit score. Shop around. Rates can vary by as much as 200%.

The cost goes up dramatically if you've had a claim in the last three years. If you don't take care of a place you rent your landlord can force you to make a claim against your insurance to pay for the damage. If something isn't working due to normal wear and tear, call your landlord and ask him to get it fixed. If you see improvements you'd like to make, call your rental agent or agency and ask if you can make them. You may get a deposit refunded or if you start making improvements that beautify your residence, you may just buy it and sell it later for much more than you initially paid. We'll talk more about that in our next book.

**LIVING EXPENSES:** For those of us who get paid every day this is the category with the biggest opportunity. When we learn to manage this and pay the rest of our bills on time, we're on our way to financial success.

Living expenses include what you spend each month for food, gas, shoes, toothpaste, haircuts, clothes, drinks after work, and even kitty litter.

Not everyone's daily living expense number is the same. Don't worry if you don't get it right the first time. I recommend starting out with $25 a day, which seems low but it can be done. It's what I started with and can always be adjusted later. Step 3 will help you validate this number.

## Step 3: Track Your Progress Daily

Unlike most of the customers you serve who get paid every week or every other week and know what's going to show up in their bank account, you get paid after every shift, the amount is variable, and it's in cash. The check we get every couple of weeks might not even buy us a drink at the bar where we work. How many times have you been handed a piece of paper with THIS IS NOT A CHECK across the front and $0.00 in the amount?

Now that you know the dollar amount of your current monthly commitment, you can start to understand and improve it using your worksheet. A good place to start is by determining if you can meet that number. The best method of proving this to yourself is to track it.

Since you're "paid" on a per shift basis, what you earn needs to be tracked at the end of every shift (or the next morning), and added against what you've spent each day, leaving your day-to-day balance. (I've tried not tracking it every day and catching up at the end of the week and it doesn't have the same effect.)  It is much easier not to leave it to guess-work.

**REELING IN THE "BARTENDER" LIFESTYLE:**  During a shift, as bartenders, we're *"ON"*.  The good ones are the ones who have developed personalities so engaging and welcoming they've cultivated a set of regulars who not only show up on a routine basis but follow them as they change bars or shifts.

At the end of a shift you're typically wound up and not ready to go home so it's easy to convince yourself there's no harm in a couple of drinks.  If you've had a good night it's nothing to spend the money you'll need next week or tomorrow at the bar where you work or at another bar.

I know after days and weeks of back-to-back shifts, my fondest desire was to have someone else serve me a drink.  It's so easy to go next door or across the street where a friend is working and pull up a stool to finally sit down for the first time all day.  But it's easy to toss a bunch of cash if you've got it sitting in your pocket.  And you're taking care of a friend, right?

We're notoriously good tippers and good souls.  When we've had a good night, we'll buy a round and when we've had a bad night, somebody will buy or treat us to a couple of drinks.

If you're still reading, there's a good possibility that you're worn out from the peaks and valleys of financial uncertainty and are ready for a change. Placing a limit on your daily expenditures and tracking them might seem elementary, but it's essential to reeling in your spending.

**TRACKING METHODS:** How you track your money is up to you. Some methods I've tried include:

**Notebook Method:** Use a lined notebook and with a line for each day. Start at the top of the page with your current balance. On each line write the date then record the shift's earnings, each expenditure, and the current balance. It's easier to carry the notebook with you and record as you spend, or you can keep your receipts and record things when you get home.

This was the first method I used and, for me, the most successful in helping me establish the habit of tracking. I kept my money in a shoebox during the week. Once a week I figured out what I would need to pay the following week and went to the bank to make a deposit or withdrawal. Worked great until I added expenses or didn't accurately track what was going in that non-skid Chuck's box.

**Calendar Method:** Either a daily or monthly calendar will also work. At the beginning of the month write the expenses that must be paid on each date, record your starting balance, then track your spending. Be careful to record each expense; no one likes an unpleasant surprise.

**Spreadsheet Method:** The spreadsheet method is the one I've found that shows me where I stand given the amount that's coming due. The advantage is it gives me the time to execute my contingency plan (explained in Step 4) if I'm going to be short.

| DATE | DAY | SHIFT | EARNINGS | EXPENSE CATEGORY | AMOUNT | BALANCE |
|---|---|---|---|---|---|---|
| | | STARTING BALANCE | | | | $1,000.00 |
| 1 | Monday | | | Rent | $675.00 | $325.00 |
| 2 | Tuesday | | | | | $325.00 |
| 3 | Wednesday | Sandbar | $93.00 | | | $418.00 |
| 4 | Thursday | | | | | $418.00 |
| 5 | Friday | Sandbar | $194.00 | Car Insurance | $162.00 | $450.00 |
| 6 | Saturday | Sandbar | $206.00 | | | $656.00 |
| 7 | Sunday | | | Weekly Expenses + Phone | $293.00 | $363.00 |
| 8 | Monday | | | | | $363.00 |
| 9 | Tuesday | | | Wifi | $53.00 | $310.00 |
| 10 | Wednesday | Sandbar | $78.00 | Car Note | $305.00 | $83.00 |
| 11 | Thursday | | | | | $83.00 |
| 12 | Friday | | | | | $83.00 |
| 13 | Saturday | Sandbar | $219.00 | | | $302.00 |
| 14 | Sunday | Sandbar | $194.00 | Weekly Expenses | $175.00 | $321.00 |
| 15 | Monday | | | | | $321.00 |
| 16 | Tuesday | | | | | $321.00 |
| 17 | Wednesday | Sandbar | $116.00 | Kohl's | $55.00 | $382.00 |
| 18 | Thursday | | | Electricity | $85.00 | $297.00 |
| 19 | Friday | Sandbar | $227.00 | | | $524.00 |
| 20 | Saturday | Sandbar | $143.00 | | | $667.00 |
| 21 | Sunday | | | Weekly Expenses | $175.00 | $492.00 |
| 22 | Monday | | | | | $492.00 |
| 23 | Tuesday | | | Renter's Insurance | $36.00 | $456.00 |
| 24 | Wednesday | Sandbar | $96.00 | | | $552.00 |
| 25 | Thursday | | | | | $552.00 |
| 26 | Friday | | | | | $552.00 |
| 27 | Saturday | Sandbar | $203.00 | | | $755.00 |
| 28 | Sunday | Sandbar | $196.00 | Weekly Expenses | $175.00 | $776.00 |
| 29 | Monday | | | | | $776.00 |
| 30 | Tuesday | | | Water | $35.00 | $741.00 |
| 31 | Wednesday | Sandbar | $102.00 | | | $843.00 |
| | | ENDING BALANCE | | | | $843.00 |

What's shown here is an example of a fully completed spreadsheet for a month whose first day was Monday.

In this example, at the end of the previous month there was a balance of $1,000. As shift earnings were recorded the balance goes up, and as expenses are paid it bring your balance down immediately. (NOTE: The column labeled *SHIFT* is there to let you keep track of what you earned on different shifts or different jobs.) Each day's earnings were entered, as were each day's expenses.

You'll notice that every Sunday there's a *"Weekly Expense"* entry for $175. This is the $25 per day mentioned in Step 2 for gas, food, entertainment, etc. This $175 is the amount of money that goes into your wallet at the beginning of the week. Before it's all gone you know you'd better fill up your gas tank and shop for enough food for the week.

So, I could tell from this spreadsheet that with a starting balance on the first of $1,000, that by working only 13 shifts and covering all my expenses, I spent $157.00 more than I made that month. I knew that I could either pick up an extra shift or two the next month, or could reduce my weekly expenditures if I wanted my cash reserve to grow. If I hadn't kept track, I could have worked all year at that rate and been more broke at the end than I was at the start. This demonstrates the value of tracking your money.

When you first start this, you might not have the $175 to put aside for the week's expenses or to pay what's coming up for the week. Step 4: Develop Your Contingency Plan will address that.

## Step 4: Develop Your Contingency Plan

Now that you know what your monthly and daily numbers are and are monitoring your progress against them, you can adjust what you're doing to be able to meet these numbers. Like most of us, there are great shifts where we make our daily number, but we also have shifts when we don't.

Additionally, bartending is seasonal. It only takes one year to figure that out. The $600 you were making every night during one season can disappear when the weather starts to cool or a new competing bar opens, and unless you've planned for that inevitability, you can get into trouble quickly.

It comes down to simple math. If what you have coming in doesn't equal what you have going out, you need to do something about it.

Your contingency plan will evolve as you learn what will work financially to fill your monetary gap.

You can start by making the folks you work with aware that you're not making your number and that you're available for extra shifts. Either be specific about which shifts or plan on picking up anything and the extra expenses you'll accrue. Always schedule at least one day off, be it to take care of business or just relax or enjoy a cookout with your friends.

A word of advice from my personal experience here: *Before you talk with your team, make sure your performance has been stellar.* This includes being on time for every shift, having a great attitude no matter what, not criticizing your boss or the owners and being a good teammate. Believe me, I know it can be tough when you're not making your number, but it's essential if you want the money shifts plus extras. And always being appreciative never hurts.

If this is not what you've been doing, change your performance now. You'll be surprised how quickly the change will be noticed. Wait until your boss comments on the change (to you or someone else), then broach the topic with him or her, admitting you recognized you could do better and made the change so you're available if he needs anything covered.

Next, write out your weekly schedule and figure out what hours you have available to do extra work. Another word of caution here, don't make the mistake I've made of trying to work seven days a week to make that number. Even when you're not making your number, if you try to do this, in the long term you end up neglecting other parts of your life, not getting enough rest, and can end up with a cold or flu which can put you completely out of commission. It eventually catches up to you and the thing you neglect may be something crucial.

I recall working in a busy bar in Plano, Texas. Not only was I the only male bartender, but I was also one of the closers four to five nights a week. I was making good money, had a very, let's say "active" social life, and enjoyed the atmosphere and vibe of the job. One morning I woke up super-sick, but ever since receiving a no-call, no-show write-up fourteen years before when I called in with no voice, I've gone to work rain or shine, sick or healthy. The bar allowed the smoking of cigarettes and cigars, and as I kept working, even with being a smoker, I felt worse and my cough got worse. After two and a half months of this, I had a day I was scheduled to open and close, but while trying to shave and shower I began coughing up a bunch of blood. I sent out an SOS text to the girls and one of them was kind enough to cover me. I went to the doctor for the first time in years; turns out I'd been working and serving people drinks and food for over two months while suffering from walking pneumonia and acute bronchitis.

I bring this up because 1) there's no telling how many people I got sick; 2) my per-shift money suffered because I wasn't on point; and 3) I felt like I had to keep working because I wasn't keeping track of my money and my bills. I was always afraid I didn't have enough to cover my expenses. If I'd been smart and kept track, I could've easily taken a day or two off and gotten better. It's time I wasted in this fashion that made me think writing this book was a good idea and would help other folks just like you who are running in a similar cycle.

To develop your contingency plan, start by making a list of all the things you can do that require little or no investment other than the time it takes to perform those tasks.

Your list of examples might include:
    Dog Walking
    Pet Sitting
    Baby Sitting
    Cleaning (Apartments, Homes, Bars, Restaurants, Offices, Gyms)
    Lawn Mowing (You'll need a lawnmower, edger, and blower – so some investment is needed)
    Driving for Uber or Lyft (You'll need a clean vehicle and good driving record)

There's so many opportunities if you're willing to invest the time and take pride in your work. Now let everyone you meet know you're available and when. You can have some inexpensive business cards printed up with a list of services and your phone number to give out when someone shows interest. You'll be surprised how quickly you can build a steady clientele and an alternate source of income.

If your contingency work starts to grow into a regular source of income, go down to the county office and register your work as a business. You'll also want to get a tax identification number and begin to keep track of your earnings and expenditures.

Make sure that what you're charging is not below or above what other people providing the same service are charging. Go online and shop for each service then set your price accordingly.

Depending upon what you're doing, you will also want to be certain you are bonded and have liability insurance that covers you. As someone who's always resented paying the cost of any type of insurance, I finally came to the realization that avoiding the cost of a lawsuit and letting customers know you're insured and bonded up front is worth it.

For more on starting your own business, I recommend **$1,000 Start-Ups** by my co-author, Leah Ward-Lee, which is available at www.amazon.com. She walks you through every facet of being a first-time business owner and makes it easy (and potentially very profitable) to pursue things that interest you other than the bar life.

# Step 5: Tame the Paper Tiger

This is one of those "I'll get to it later" habits that can really get you in trouble if you don't put in place a method of managing it.

**SET UP A PAPERWORK MANAGEMENT SYSTEM:** I use the folder system. You can do this even if you don't have a file cabinet by using a simple banker's box that you can pick up for a couple of dollars at an office supply or any big box store.

While you're there pick up a box of hanging folders that come with plastic labels. The paper inserts that go in the labels make it easy to label each one.

At the front of the box I have a folder marked "bills" where I put unpaid bills until I pay them. The second folder is marked "action". This is where I put everything I need to do.

**KEEP A "TO DO" LIST:** Like any other tool, there are many methods of managing the things you need to do. For most of us, if we don't have a written list it's easy to forget to do something that either ends up costing us time or money.

If you haven't been keeping a list or haven't been using it as a tool to keep track of everything you need to take care of, start by listing everything you can think of that needs to get done.

Next, prioritize the list. The best method I've found is "The Eisenhower" method. Eisenhower commanded more than two million soldiers during World War II and developed this method of prioritizing his work.

Categorize each task on your 'to do' list based upon its importance and urgency and put it into the Eisenhower Box by answering the following: (graphic and explanation from www.thousandinsights.files.wordpress.com)

- Is this task important or not important?
- Is this task urgent or not urgent?

|  | Urgent | Not Urgent |
|---|---|---|
| **Important** | Crying Baby<br>Kitchen Fire<br>Some Calls<br><br>**Do**  ①  | ② Exercise<br>Vocation<br>Planning<br><br>**Plan** |
| **Not Important** | ③<br>Interruptions<br>Distractions<br>Other Calls<br><br>**Delegate** | ④<br>Trivia<br>Busy Work<br>Time Wasters<br><br>**Drop** |

Priority 1 tasks are both urgent and important. These tasks need to be addressed personally and immediately. However, if you're spending most of your time on these tasks, you're just putting out fires. This is usually an indicator that you're merely reactive and are not managing your priorities and actions ahead of time.

Priority 2 tasks are important but not urgent. These tasks need to be addressed personally but not immediately so they need to have a planned date. Give them a start date and a completion date. This will help you build your activity plan/calendar. Ideally, most of your tasks should be priority 2 tasks.

Priority 3 tasks are urgent but not important, so they require immediate attention, but not necessarily by you. These tasks are usually other people's priorities, not yours. If possible, delegate them, if not, move them to a Priority 4.

Priority 4 tasks are not urgent or important, so they're mostly a waste of time. These tasks should be dropped as they provide no value.

We'll talk more about managing your 'to do' list during Step 6: Hold a Weekly Business Meeting, so for now just focus on making sure everything you need to do is on your list and categorized.

**OPEN AND SORT YOUR MAIL:** Put all the mail you've received this week and any mail you haven't dealt with in the past in a pile and quickly sort it into three piles. Pile 1 is junk mail. Pile 2 is mail addressed to you that you recognize requires action or that you have to open to figure out why it was sent to you and determine if it requires action on your part. Pile 3 is the stack of periodicals or items you want to read later that require no action on your part.

Now that your mail is in stacks it's easier and less time consuming to deal with.

**GET RID OF THE MUDA:** Next, deal with Pile 1. Throw every piece of junk mail that doesn't have your name and address on it into the recycle bin. (At my brother's last place, the mailboxes were centralized and there was a recycle bin so he could do this sort when he picked up his mail and not even bring it into the house.)

If the mail has your name and address on it, tear it up small enough to require a lot of work to tape it back together or shred it. Identity theft is way too time consuming to deal with.

**REDUCE THE BACKLOG OF PERIODICALS:** Now deal with Pile 3.

When I separated all the paperwork I had in my condo my stack of periodicals was life threatening (particularly to my cat Mylo and she's a big cat).

I took a hard look at it and realized I probably didn't need to keep last year's issues of *Consumer Reports* since the information was obsolete. I easily dumped fifty pounds of periodicals whose information was out of date or that I'd never look at again.

Take a hard look at what you've been saving. Is it worth the space you're giving it? Is the information available somewhere else? If so, get rid of it.

**MAIL ADDRESSED TO YOU:** Open each piece and sort it into Bills, Action, and Information piles. If you find any junk mail, rip it up and get rid of it.

**Bills:** Pay the bills that are on your budget for next week. If you're lucky enough to be ahead of plan, this month you can also pay any installment load or credit card bills that came in early. This allows you to take advantage of the extra number of days in your billing cycle when your balance was lower.

Put your bills that aren't due in the upcoming week in your Bill's folder. You'll review these each week during your weekly business meeting.

**Actions:** Now go through the stack that requires action on your part. Categorize each item into one of the four categories and add them to your "to do" list.

If you find something that's both urgent and important to take care of now and can make time to place the call or pay the bill – take action.

**Information:** We all receive mail I categorize as "information". These are things like special offers, sales, or things that are sent, usually to get us to do something. This stack can easily get out of hand. Put these in one stack and put them somewhere where you usually have a few minutes every day to read. I give these a shelf life of one week and toss last week's when I do my weekly mail sort.

# Step 6: Hold a Weekly Business Meeting

The nicest thing you can do for yourself is to use your day off to take care of the business of running your life. Most successful businesses have a weekly meeting where results are reviewed and the next week is planned. The business of running a successful life is no different.

Setting one day a week to take care of these things that keep your life running smoothly significantly reduces your stress because it prevents "emergencies" that happen because we didn't take the time to prevent them.

If you consider all the hours you spend doing one thing while worrying about something you're not doing, you get what I mean. Right now, the luxury, and it might seem like a luxury, of taking a whole day off for yourself might be out of reach, but you can get there incrementally.

**<u>SET A DAY AND START TIME:</u>** Even if the first time you can only carve out an hour or two, set a day and time, then set an alarm for that time.

I find that by not only setting the day, but also setting the time, I'm motivated get out of bed, particularly when all I'd really like to do is sleep. As weeks go on you'll find you have been sub-consciously preparing for your meeting all week.

**MAKE WISE USE OF THIS TIME:** Turn off the ringer and automatic notifications on your cellphone. To be effective you've got to be able to focus.

If you've got something that can be happening in the background - like washing a load of laundry or a running the dishwasher – get these started and on auto-pilot.

It's important to manage your time during the "weekly meeting" process. You want to get through all three of the activities: meeting preparation, financial progress review, and actions during the meeting time so you have some time for yourself.

**Activity 1: Preparation.** Get everything you're going to need in one, uncluttered place. Make sure you have an empty trash can to throw away everything you're going to discard and, if you recycle, all the paper you'll be tossing.

If you have mail that's come in since you initially sorted, process it first so you have an up-to-date and prioritized "to do" list and current bills and action items.

If your bank statement came in this week, either electronically or on paper, reconcile it with your budget. Nothing is worse than making decisions based upon a bank balance that doesn't match what you thought it was.

**Activity 2: Financial Progress Review.** Start by reviewing where you are against where you need to be. Pull out your monthly budget, and if the month is more than half over, also use next month's projection, and review where you are against what you're going to need for the next several weeks. Are you on track or do you need to spend time in the week to come executing your contingency plan?

Even though you've been keeping up with this daily, this is your time to look forward while you have enough time to prevent getting into trouble.

**Activity 3: Take Action.**

- **Pay your bills.** Pay the bills that need to be paid for the upcoming week and fund your weekly expenses.

- **Work down your "to do" list.** First, take care of the

urgent and important items on your "to do" list. Then look at items that are important, but will become urgent if you don't take care of them this week and take care of them.

- **Update your "to do" list.** I've found that creating a new "to do" list helps me put together my plan for the week. I used to labor under the misperception that one magic day everything on my list would be done.

Once I realized that there would always be more to do and that by managing the things that I had to do and getting them done it left me more time to do what I wanted to do. I've found this preferable than spending any of my time or money doing damage control on things I should have done.

- **Clean Your Space and Do Your Laundry:** Why, you might ask, is there a section during a weekly business meeting for cleaning my space? Because, time is money and it takes less time to keep a place clean if we do it every week than if we do it when it gets so bad we can't stand it.

It also takes less time to keep our stuff well organized than it does to waste time looking for things we can't find or figuring out you're out of clean socks when you are getting ready for a shift.

No one likes to come home to or wake up to a dirty place. Taking an hour a week to clean your place so the bathroom, kitchen, and bedroom are clean reduces stress and it's much easier to keep it clean than it is to get it clean when you don't.

- **Run Your Errands:** Plan out the route you're going to take and set off to do all your errands in one trip. You'll find going to the bank, grocery store, and gas station only once a week, rather than every day helps your money go a lot further.

Convenience stores co-located with gas stations typically charge quite a premium for grocery items. You pay a high cost for that "convenience".

This is also your time to stop and get the pair of jeans, shoes, or new shirt you need. Establish a habit of buying what you need when you need it in weekly increments rather than by going on a spending spree when you've had a great week.

**PERSONAL TIME:** Once you've had your business meeting you can enjoy your personal time knowing you're prepared for next week. You can just put your feet up and relax, or take some time to check email and maybe Facebook your friends and regulars that you appreciate them and look forward to seeing them soon.

## Step 7: Raise Your Credit Score

**WHY YOUR CREDIT SCORE IS IMPORTANT:** During Step 2: Analyze Your Monthly Commitment, I mentioned the cost of credit (interest rates) as one of the reasons your credit score is important; however, that's only the tip of the iceberg.

The rate you pay for your car insurance, renter's insurance, and even your health insurance is affected by your credit score. Insurance companies carefully guard the method they use to calculate their rates; however, a portion of the calculation is based on your FICO score.

Utility companies often base the amount of deposit you're required to pay based upon your FICO score.

Employers also have the ability, typically with your permission, to check your credit score and use it, particularly when you're being considered for a management position.

Your FICO score is also considered when you want to rent an apartment, or buy a home or car.

**HOW IT'S CALCULATED:** According to the Experian website (https://www.experian.com/blogs/ask-experian/how-is-a-fico-score-calculated/), FICO (formerly Fair, Isaac and Company) is a credit scoring company that produces FICO credit scores. The algorithms/formulas used to calculate FICO scores are proprietary to them. However, like all other credit scores, FICO scores are calculated using the information in your credit report.

FICO scores weigh five types of information from your credit report in the calculation:

**Payment history** is by far the most important factor in credit scores. It is essential to pay your bills on time, every time. Any late payment is going to have a significant effect on credit scores. Your payment history accounts for about 35 percent of a credit score.

**Utilization,** which is the balance-to-limit ratio on your credit cards, is the second most important criteria in credit scores. You never want a balance to be higher than 30 percent of the credit limit on a single credit card or the total of all your cards.

To determine your utilization rate, add up your balances and all your credit limits and divide the total of your balances by the total of your limits. This percentage should not be more than 30 percent as a maximum. The lower your utilization, the better.

Ideally, you should pay your balances in full each month. People with the best credit scores have zero late payments and utilization rates of less than 10 percent. Your utilization rate accounts for about 30 percent of your credit score.

The first two factors account for two-thirds of your score. Paying your bills on time and keeping your balances low on your credit cards are essential to having good credit scores. The other elements in a credit score build on those first two:

**Length of credit history** is based on the length of time each account has been open and how long it has been since you used certain accounts. A longer credit history can increase your credit scores. Length of history accounts for approximately 15 percent of a FICO score.

**Recent activity** looks at how much new credit you have applied for in the past three to six months. Applications for credit are shown as new inquiries. Recent credit isn't limited to inquiries, though. It also includes paying off accounts, whether accounts have become delinquent or have been brought current, and whether account balances have increased or decreased significantly. Recent credit accounts for 10 percent of a FICO score.

**Credit mix** refers to the different kinds of accounts you have including mortgages, credit cards, auto loans, and other installment loans. Having a variety of credit types can help increase your score slightly, but you should not apply for several accounts all at once to try to improve this element. Doing so will likely do more harm than good because of the impact on recent credit activity. Instead, use credit wisely and you will naturally build a good mix of credit types over time. The mix of various types of credit accounts for 10 percent of a FICO score.

**YOUR CREDIT REPORT:** In the United States, Equifax, Experian, and TransUnion are the three major agencies that provide credit reports. Although they are similar, each calculates your credit score in a slightly different way and as such your scores can be different.

Additionally, not all lenders are required to report to all three credit bureaus, so accounts that are considered by one of the agencies in calculating your score might not be included in the others. Since you typically don't know which bureau a new creditor or insurance company is going to use it is important to consider your scores with all three.

You're entitled to a free credit report from each agency annually and any time you are turned down for credit. There are also online services that will provide you with your scores and a synopsis of your credit history; however, these companies are in the business of selling you all types of services. They'll tell you what the best credit cards are, file taxes for you, and tempt you to buy services you may or may not need.

**CREDIT REPAIR SCAMS:** There are online companies who, for a fee, promise to repair your credit rating. What they do for you is nothing you can't do for yourself. If you need to have your credit repaired the money you're going to pay them is much better spent paying down your debt.

**REPAIR YOUR CREDIT:** Repairing your credit takes a commitment, but, quite frankly, the effort isn't difficult and over the course of a year you'll find it reduces what you pay for your insurance, interest, and penalties by at least 10%.

This 10% raise is free money, yours for the taking.

**Personal Information.** The personal information in your report includes your name and all the derivatives you've ever used. It also includes every address you've had and all your employment information.

Sometimes reporting gets mixed up and a different name, address, or job can show up on your credit report. You can correct this information to keep your records up to date. While frustrating, it likely won't be as high impact as other potential errors.

**Tradelines or Credit Accounts.** This lists all the accounts each credit bureau has that are attributable to you.

Check to insure the accounts listed on your report belong to you. It's not uncommon to find an account listed on your report that isn't yours, particularly if you have a common name. If you're dealing with this, file a dispute right away. If you believe the wrong account may indicate identity theft, you may want to consider placing a security freeze or fraud alert on your credit reports right away.

Additionally, you may find missing or inaccurate account information. Check to be certain there aren't accounts listed on your credit report that should or shouldn't have "fallen off" by now. Check to see if your account payment history and the reported balances and credit limits are correct. It's not uncommon for lenders to make reporting errors.

**Credit Inquiries** are also on your report. Hard inquiries are the ones that affect your score and can occur when lenders, employers, landlords and others request your credit report. Your authorization is needed when an employer checks your credit report, but isn't necessarily needed for other reasons such as account monitoring by your existing lenders or in response to a legal order. Shopping around for loan offers (buying a vehicle) often results in multiple inquiries listed on your report, but some scoring models group them together so that multiple inquiries for the same type of loan count as one within a certain time period.

**Collection Accounts.** Collection accounts may appear multiple times because collection accounts can be sold or transferred several times, which can result in the same account being listed more than once with different collection agencies. In this situation, your credit report should list which accounts were sold or transferred (normally listed as closed) and which are current and open. The multiple entries may look like an error, but can be correct if the statuses are up to date.

**Public Records** including foreclosures, and civil judgments can stay on your credit report for seven years. Bankruptcies can stay on your report for as long as ten years.
This information is contained in public records filed in a county, state or federal materials that are generally available to the public. Examples of public records that are often included in credit reports include bankruptcies, civil judgments and foreclosures.

Any proof you have such as a W2 for missing employment or a lease for a missing address will speed the correction.

Inaccurate reporting regarding an account typically should be addressed with the creditor first in writing. Typically, creditors are responsive because they don't want inaccurate reporting either.

Once you have a satisfactory response from a creditor, forward that to the credit bureau(s) along with a letter asking that the information be corrected.

First and foremost, while you're working on this you can't miss or be even one day late on any payments.

Second, you don't want to throw money away that you need by overdrawing your account. Even being a day late or a dollar short for an automated payment will cost you at least $35.

Third, if you have any pending collections you haven't addressed, contact that collection agency and make arrangements to pay them.

Remember, this is a negotiation. These agencies typically buy collections for much less than the amount owed. Your original creditor already wrote off the loan and probably won't be offering you credit any time soon. That's history and you typically can't change the past; however, that's not the case for the collection agency.

What you want is for the account to be marked as closed and paid according to the negotiated terms for the lowest amount possible and in the least time possible so it can start aging off your credit report and be replaced with a better credit history.

Fourth, defer any major purchases or changes in insurance companies. If possible, don't take any actions that require credit inquiries. You'll pay more now or run the risk of being turned down – both affect that magic FICO number.

Although it's tempting to go after the car, if your credit score is low, you might be better served to work on one of your credit cards.

When you get that account down to a zero balance call the company and ask them to raise your limit. Keep charging on the account and paying it on time when it's due. When I started this, I selected the credit card I used for gas and groceries. Every time I use the card I put that amount of cash in an envelope. When the bill arrived, I took the cash to the bank, deposited it, then paid the bill.

I literally saw my credit score go up a few points every month as a result.

Pick the second account and pay it off. When I did this, I picked the account with the lowest balance, but selected one that I used frequently so I wouldn't risk them closing the account which would have reduced my overall available credit score.

Once you get your credit score out of the danger zone, you can slowly start applying for additional accounts, one at a time, while working to get to a zero balance on every account.

**Activity 7: Monitor Your Credit Score and Renegotiate Your Rates.** Credit scores are broken into tiers. When your credit score moves up from one tier to the next the rates you pay for loans, credit cards, and insurance go down.

Understanding those tiers and the implications of each gives you the tools you need to negotiate better rates. (https://www.sapling.com)

- **Tier One.** Tier one credit scores are generally regarded as scores that range from 760 to 850. Since tiers include a range of scores, a FICO score of 760 is essentially the same as 850 and will get you the same rates as a score of 850, according to Bankrate.com. A score of 850 is more of a status symbol than anything else. Tier one credit scores qualify for the best interest rates possible, and are typically the only tier that qualifies for the "Special" interest rates of 0.0 percent for auto loans.

- **Tier Two.** Tier Two credit scores range from 700 to 759. Any FICO score falling within the tier two range is still regarded as very good credit. Consumers with tier two credit scores will normally receive an interest rate that's a step down from the top interest rate. Anyone with a tier two credit score should have no problem qualifying for loans or credit cards.

- Tier three credit scores range from 660 to 699. Having a credit score fall in the range of 660 to 699 is indicative of good credit. Consumers with Tier three FICO scores will generally have no problem qualifying for loans or credit cards, although they will not receive the best interest rate.

- **Tier Four.** Scores that range from 620 to 659 qualify as tier four credit scores, also known as "Average" credit. Like the above tiers, someone with a tier four credit score will usually qualify for loans and credit cards, but financial institutions take a much longer and in-depth look at the person's financial history.

- **Tier Five.** A credit score that falls between 580 and 619 will place a person in the tier five credit score. People that have a credit score between 580 and 619 are considered "subprime" by lenders. Qualifying for a loan becomes difficult in the tier five range, and many lenders require either a co-signer or collateral before approving a loan for someone that has a tier five credit score. Interest rates will also jump up dramatically for anyone considered subprime. A person with a tier five credit score can expect to pay two or more percentage points higher than the average rate.

Using Bankrate.com's January 2018, national average 30-year fixed mortgage interest rate of 4.97 percent, a person with a tier five credit score will typically pay at least 6.97 percent or more. So, for a $200,000 house, you're paying $13,900 more for the loan. $14k of your money gone just because of your credit score? That's a lot of shifts!

- **Tier Six.** According to Bankrate.com, tier six is the lowest tier that will qualify anyone for a mortgage rate. Tier six credit scores range from 500 to 579. People with a tier six credit score will qualify for the highest legal interest rate, if they qualify at all. Most banks will require collateral or a co-signer before approving any loans.

You knew your credit score was important, now you know why. Let's start on the fun stuff.

# Step 8: Build Long-Term Wealth

**GET STARTED AS SOON AS POSSIBLE:** The numbers below tell the story. Putting away $100 a month for the next 10 years gives you back $14,774, a profit of $2,774 more than you invested. That, on the surface, doesn't sound like a great deal. The same amount invested over a longer period compounds what you earn without increasing the amount of your investment.

| Amount | Interest Rate | Years | Value | Months | Amount Invested | Profit |
|--------|---------------|-------|-----------|--------|-----------------|---------|
| $100   | 4%            | 10    | $14,774   | 120    | $12,000         | $2,774  |
| $100   | 4%            | 20    | $36,800   | 240    | $24,000         | $12,800 |
| $100   | 4%            | 30    | $69,636   | 360    | $36,000         | $33,636 |
| $100   | 4%            | 40    | $118,590  | 480    | $48,000         | $70,590 |

**APPLY THE 10% RULE:** If you work toward saving at least 10% of what you earn and make reasonable financial decisions, you'll be well on your way to building long-term wealth. The more you have socked away, particularly if it's invested and not growing mold in your sock drawer, the more financial leverage you have.

This leverage gives you opportunities you wouldn't otherwise have.

It's always been one of life's ironies that once you don't need to borrow money, there are banks lined up trying to lend it to you.

Once you have your short-term emergency fund established and you're working down your debt, you can start to use the 10% rule to build your long-term wealth.

**401k:** With our current tax laws, putting money into your 401k reduces what you GIVE to the government. In 2018 the annual amount you can contribute to your 401k is $18,500 a year. This translates to whatever the amount you can put away in your 401k up to $18,500 reduces the total taxable income the government recognizes by that amount. Since you're taxed on a percentage basis this not only reduces the taxable amount, but can also reduce your tax rate if it takes you to the lower tax bracket.

You can look at it like this: when a guest gives you a dollar, instead of tipping out and then paying tax on the dollar before you take it home, you get to keep the whole dollar and earn interest on it.

Most employers no longer give a 401k match; however, if yours does, why would you turn down free money? Even if the employer only matches a percent of what you're able to put in your 401k, why wouldn't you make the commitment and have them pay you that bonus?

Here's the one rule about your 401k you need to understand: taking money out of it is not only taxed, but has a penalty. You can borrow from it, but you will pay the penalty if you don't declare it as a loan and pay it back within the time allotted, which is usually before the end of the tax year.

**SAVINGS ACCOUNTS:** Savings accounts typically don't pay very much interest, however, they're where you want to store your emergency fund and the money you're saving for a particular purpose, such as a down payment for a car or tuition. Therefore, this is not the repository you're going to use to build your long-term wealth.

Before you open an account, be sure you understand where you're putting your money and the rules for taking it out. Check the following:

**The Interest Rate:** Go online and research by typing in "Savings Account Interest Rates". Currently rates are between .10% and 1.5% annually. Even if you only have $10 in your account you might as well get paid for letting the bank use it. If your current checking account gives you free checking because you have a savings account with the same bank, find out how much you have to keep in your savings account to qualify for free checking, don't put in a dollar more, and don't withdraw down below that level.

It goes without saying that you don't want to pay bank fees, not even ATM fees, ever. They're ridiculously inflated and have become a huge revenue source for banks. An easy way around this is to schedule one or two bank trips a week and only use your weekly allotted cash to make any purchases. This saves time, you stay within your budget, and there's no more giving away the $2.50 or $3.00 it costs to have access to your own money.

**No Minimum Balance and No Hidden Fees:** You also want a savings account without a minimum balance and with no hidden fees.

**No Transaction Fees:** Some accounts have transaction fees. Look for an account without fees. (Often these limit the number of withdrawals per month and then charge a fee if you exceed that limit.)

**No Minimum Deposit to Open:** Make certain if there is a minimum deposit you know what it is and whether there's a penalty if your balance dips below it.

**FDIC Insurance Up to The Maximum Allowed by Law:** Be certain that the account is insured by The Federal Deposit Insurance Corporation (FDIC) up to the maximum, which is currently $250,000, allowed by law. This is essential and protects you from a bank going bankrupt, which has happened more often than we'd like to think.

**Link Directly to Any Existing Bank Account:** This is a convenience; however, it's also a great way to transfer money back and forth.

**Based in the United States of America:** You are welcome to use a foreign bank; however, be prepared to declare that and the amount you have in the bank on your tax return. There are serious penalties if you don't.

**INVESTMENTS:** How you invest is as important as where you invest. Unless you're a full-time investor who monitors your investments on a daily basis, understanding and using the practice of dollar cost averaging is important. If you select an investment that has a solid history of growth and monitor it for large fluctuations every month, it's typically less risky to put a set amount into the investment each month. This allows you to purchase a smaller amount when the value of the investment goes up and a larger amount when the investment goes down.

**Stock:** Since most of us weren't officers at Facebook or Microsoft and entitled to stock options when they went public, choosing to invest in stock of individual companies requires a strategy and the willingness to invest your time to do the research.

There are numerous articles on Wikihow that will give you advice on how to understand what a company's numbers indicate. You can learn about companies who are publicly traded by contacting their investor relations department. Typically, contact information is available on their website. Four basic numbers can give you a general idea of how a company is doing:

- **P/E (price to earnings ratio)** - a negative ratio may suggest that the company isn't profitable

- **EBIDTA (Earnings before interest, depreciation, tax, and amortization)** is a method of measuring net income with much of the accounting already taken into consideration. EBIDTA is sometimes called operational cash flow and shows what portion of a company's revenue could actually be spent on expenses.

- **Free Cash Flow** represents money that the company has to pursue opportunities that may increase their stock's value.

- **Debt Ratio** is a percentage of the company's total debts against assets.

One thing to understand is that publicly traded companies sometimes make short-term decisions to protect their stock price, particularly if they are involved in a merger or acquisition.

It's important to consider the company's market share, competitive position, and the external factors that affect the industry of your companies of interest.

Additionally, you need to be aware of and consider the indices that affect market behavior such as consumer confidence and unemployment.

It's easy to purchase stock. You can buy it directly from the company you're investing in or through a full-service or online broker.

**Mutual Funds:** When you buy shares in a mutual fund, you can usually be certain of some level of diversification in your investment holdings. This is true because instead of purchasing stock from one company you're buying a portion of a fund that may own hundreds of different stocks. When one stock in the portfolio performs poorly, other well-performing stocks can offset the disadvantage. Since mutual funds can own many types of asset classes, a single investment has the potential to provide all the diversification that an investor needs.

While building a diversified portfolio of individual stocks and bonds requires a large outlay of capital, mutual funds are accessible by just about everyone because they can be purchased with small dollar amounts. Most people have a need to invest, but they may not have the expertise to invest wisely. A mutual fund often places investment decisions in the hands of a professional money manager. With the goal of increasing value and managing risk, the fund manager decides what investments to buy and sell. (Extracted from: http://www.mutual funds.about.com)

Erik Tyson, author of the Mutual Funds for Dummies books, observed that mutual funds "offer a low-cost method of investing in bonds and stocks, and you get a professional, full-time fund manager on your team." (http://www.dummies.com/personal-finance/investing/mutual-funds/mutual-funds-for-dummies-cheat-sheet/ summarized from Mutual Funds For Dummies, 7th Edition By Eric Tyson)

He also advises that when you get ready to make this type of investment you should take the time to understand the type of funds that are available, invest in a stable fund, and select a fund that has low fees.

**US Treasury:** There are a multitude of investment products issued by the federal government. Most are low risk; however, the interest rates are low relative to what you can earn with higher risk investments.

- **Treasury Bills**, or T-bills, are typically issued at a discount from the par amount (also called face value). For example, if you buy a $1,000 bill at a price per $100 of $99.986111, then you'll pay $999.86 ($1,000 x .99986111 = $999.86111). When the bill matures, you'll be paid its face value, $1,000. Your interest is the face value minus the purchase price. It is possible for a bill auction to result in a price equal to par, which means that Treasury will issue and redeem the securities at par value.

- **Treasury Notes** or T-notes, are issued in terms of 2, 3, 5, 7, and 10 years, and pay interest every six months until they mature. The price of a note may be greater than, less than, or equal to the face value of the note. When a note matures, you are paid its face value.

- **Treasury Bonds** are issued in terms of 30 years and pay interest every six months until they mature. When a Treasury bond matures, you are paid its face value. The price and yield of a Treasury bond are determined at auction. The price may be greater than, less than, or equal to the face value of the bond.

- **Floating Rate Notes** (FRNs). The U.S. Treasury began issuing Floating Rate Notes (FRNs) in January 2014. The securities have a term of two years. The price of an FRN may be greater than, less than, or equal to the face value of the security. When an FRN matures, you are paid its face value.

- **EE bonds** earn the same rate of interest (a fixed rate) for up to 30 years. When you buy the bond, you know what rate of interest it will earn. Treasury announces the rate every May 1 and November 1 for new EE bonds.

- **I Bonds** earn interest based on combining a fixed rate and an inflation rate that can and usually does change twice a year.

(More in-depth information on each type and how to purchase is available at [https://www.treasurydirect.gov](https://www.treasurydirect.gov), which was the source for this information.)

**REAL PROPERTY:** Home ownership is often not viewed as within reach by the majority of those in our business, which can be shortsighted. Whether it's a single-family home, townhouse, or condominium, if the property is reasonably maintained, the property value typically rises. (This excludes mobile homes and timeshares.)

Saving a down payment can be a formidable undertaking; however, often while you're saving, an opportunity to rent to own or owner financing might become available. A simple rule of thumb is to plan on a 20% down payment and 80% mortgage. Typical mortgages include the principal, interest, tax, and insurance. Once the mortgage is satisfied the owner receives the deed and takes over the tax and insurance.

To qualify for a mortgage your credit history and your current income will be considered. The sum of your annual income minus the cost of any annual debt times 2.5 is typically the amount a lender will loan you for a mortgage.

The monthly cost of home ownership can be as low or even lower than the cost of renting and, as long as you make your payments, you'll eventually own the home.

You're probably familiar with the mantra of wise real estate selection that reads: location, location, location when it comes to resale value, so consider the location carefully before you buy.

I remember working a 358-workday year, which meant that although I finished the year with the equivalent of one week off, I cleared well over $100k. I thought about buying a new truck or taking a vacation, but after looking at rental prices on homes and apartments, I took $57k of that and bought a condo. After the initial investment, my entire expenses for owning a 2-bedroom, 2-bathroom condo were $252 a month for the HOA, $48 a month for insurance, $50 a month for an appliance maintenance policy, $100 a month put aside for property taxes, and a variable electric bill. For less than $700 a month, I owned property much larger than most of my friends' and coworkers' apartments and my credit rating kept going up. Fast forward almost six years and it's currently worth $114k flat if I wanted a one-tine cash infusion, or I can rent it out for $1150 a month, pay the HOA, insurance, appliance maintenance policy, put

$100 a month aside for the taxes, and another $100 for any repairs, and pocket $500 a month for doing virtually nothing. The choice is rent or own and if you can afford it, I highly advise owning. And I'll admit, it felt damn good to have some property with my name on it.

To get the best rate on a mortgage you should have a Tier 1 credit score and a 20% down payment; however, there are mortgage companies who will finance a mortgage even when you don't meet either criteria  If interest rates are rising, your income is at least 2.5 times what you need to borrow, and rent in your area is higher that a mortgage would be it might be a good mover to buy ow.

Once you pay down your existing debt the alternate source of income you identified in Step 4 can be the best method of saving your down payment. Think about it: $500 a month in alternate income is $6000 in a year.

# Step 9: Plan Your Next Chapter

If being a bartender is what you want to do with your life, then following Steps 1-8 will help ensure you're financially stable; however, many bartenders and people in the food service business would really prefer to eventually do something else.

Many bartenders start out in this business part-time only to look up and find ten or fifteen years have passed and they're still where they started. Often, unfortunately, they've started down the path of making a transition several times and abandoned their dreams or put them on hold. It's hard to let solid, easy money go right?

If this sounds like you, what do you want your next chapter to be? Regardless of whether you want it to be a career change, going back to school to earn a degree, opening a new business, championing a cause, or traveling to a distant shore, you, and only you, can make that happen.

The following excerpt, from D. Razor Babb in <u>Babb's Writer's Workshop</u> challenges us to dream big:

"If you think small, then your world will be small. If you think big, then your world will be big." A simple statement and derivative of many similar statements found in self-help, philosophy and motivational texts throughout time. But, the message is timeless. It was spoken by the author of <u>The Alchemist</u>, Paulo Coelho, in an interview with Oprah Winfrey. Inspired by Hemingway's, <u>The Old Man and The Sea</u>, Coelho wrote of the Andalusian shepherd, Santiago, who after dreaming of finding treasure in the Egyptian pyramids, sells his flock and embarks on a journey of courage and intuition that is symbolic of every man and woman's journey.

<u>The Alchemist</u> wasn't initially a bestseller and Coelho's publisher lamented that it would never sell. Coelho decided that since he wrote in the book, "When you want something, all the universe will conspire in helping you achieve it," he needed to live by those words and told the publisher to give it time. Twenty-five years later, <u>The Alchemist</u> has sold 65 million copies and has been translated into

88 languages.

Coelho believes that so many people respond to Santiago's journey because everyone wants to take the same journey, but they don't get started due to fear. Most people get bogged down with the burden of struggling to earn a living and lose their dream. And, their inner child constantly nags at them, "Do you remember the dream?" Coelho's dream was to be a writer. He calls his quest a Personal Legend – the reason he or anyone exists. He advises that anyone can fill hours and days with less than meaningful things and activities, but inside we all know we have a reason for being here. If you aren't living your dream, your calling, and your inspiration, you are betraying your own Personal Legend. Recently he published his 31$^{st}$ book, Adultery.

Early in The Alchemist, Santiago is told "the world's greatest lie", that you don't control your own life – that a system, an establishment, doesn't allow you to control anything. You buy into the world's greatest lie the moment you agree to obey rules that are not your rules; when you say, "I have to." So many people say in that moment, "Am I going to be different?  Am I going to make people upset? No."

Coelho was so adamantly discouraged by his parents (growing up in Brazil) from being a writer, that when he repeatedly refused to pursue any other course they had him sent to a mental institution, three times!  At the time, Brazil was a very repressive society under military dictatorship and they were scared of everything.

He escaped and fled to New York City with only $200.00 in his pocket.  He bought Greyhound Bus trips to long-distance destinations so he'd be able to sleep on the bus and finally ended up in San Francisco during the hippie movement.  Eventually, he began earning a fairly good living by writing songs. At age 39 he decided to quit everything and pursue his Personal Legend and write full time. That's when he wrote The Alchemist, and it only took two weeks.  He says that he's not even sure 'he' wrote the book, but he is sure he was a good instrument 'for' the writing.

In the book, the alchemist tells Santiago, "Listen to your heart.  It knows all things …." Even as he meets forces beyond his control, as long as Santiago follows his true path, he knows one day he will prevail. Just as in life. Your life is yours and you choose how great it can be. Not your job, not your spouse, not the government, it's <u>your</u> life.

Coelho says, "There is a Zen proverb, 'If you want something, step aside and let it come to you.' Before a dream is realized the Soul of the World tests everything that was learned along the way. It does so not because it is evil, but so that we may master the lessons we've learned and move toward our dream. When tested, many give up or give in. The few that endure realize their dreams."

We must ask ourselves, if we were to die tomorrow, could we rest in peace knowing we were true to our dreams?

**<u>THE SMART GOAL:</u>** Decide upon your goals for the next chapter of your life. Even while working to achieve financial success, having a goal for your next chapter is not only motivating, it also helps to focus your efforts.

What are your goals for this year? Not just your professional goals, but your personal goals. In Napoleon Hill's classic, <u>Think and Grow</u>

Rich, he interviewed the most successful icons of his day and one of the conclusions he came to was that in order to be successful you have to set goals and then develop a time-based plan to reach them.

Many of us start every year making New Year's resolutions. So many of us abandon them before the end of the first month that it's become a cliché. As a result, many people decide not to set goals because they don't want to take the risk of not achieving them.

Be brave. Take a chance on yourself. Decide what your goals are then set yourself up for success by making them SMART goals. This phrase has been around for as long as any of us can remember, but how many of us structure our goals this way?

SMART goals are: Specific, Measurable, Achievable, Relevant, and Time-Based.

**Specific:** The goal has to be specific so that you avoid false starts and time wasters. If you're like I am, when I'm well rested and take the time to examine my life I can think of ten goals; however, I've learned to focus on only those I've taken the time to clearly define.

Instead of "I'm going to become a writer", which is indeed a goal, a specific goal would be: "I'm going to write, self-publish, and market a book that helps other bartenders be financially successful."

Instead of "I'm going to go back to college and get my degree", a specific goal would be: "I'm going to transfer my credits to Jacksonville Community College and earn my Associates Degree in Liberal Arts."

**Measurable:** It's important to state your goal in a manner that allows you to know what it looks like when it's done.

I've found that the tougher a goal is and the further the finish line is from where you're standing, the more important it is that you make the goal measurable.

So, my goal of "I'm going to write, self-publish, and market a book…." becomes "By April 1st I will have written, self-published and marketed The Bartender's Guide to Financial Freedom or How to Quit Being Broke and will have sold the first 12 copies." Now the goal starts to come to life.

Using that same principle "I'm going to transfer my credits to Jacksonville Community College and earn my Associate's Degree in Liberal Arts" becomes "By the end of the winter semester in December 20XX, I will have earned my Associate's Degree in Liberal Arts from Jacksonville Community College."

Since both these goals won't happen by themselves making the goal measurable forces you to develop a plan to achieve them.

**Achievable:** It's essential to believe your goal is achievable. If you don't believe you can accomplish it, you'll be tempted to abandon your goal when you hit the first roadblock.

I've found the best method for me of making a goal achievable is to write out the steps I'll have to take to achieve it and then analyze each of those steps. For example, here are the steps I wrote out to get this book into your hands:

- **Step 1:** Complete first draft of the book
- **Step 2:** Upload manuscript and complete cover
- **Step 3:** Get format approval and order proof from fulfillment provider
- **Step 4:** Join Chamber of Commerce
- **Step 5:** Develop a Marketing Plan
- **Step 6:** Register publishing business and obtain tax ID
- **Step 7:** Open business bank account
- **Step 8:** Get charge machine
- **Step 9:** Edit and upload changes to the proof
- **Step 10:** Publish the book
- **Step 11:** Order and receive copies
- **Step 12:** Publicize the book
- **Step 13:** Begin sales

Once I realized I could do this in thirteen steps, it became achievable in my mind, particularly when I realized some of those steps involved waiting for someone else to do something. For example, Step 3. I realized that while I was waiting for the proof to come in the mail I could start working on Steps 4-8.

The goal of earning an Associate's Degree in Liberal Arts from Jacksonville Community College by the winter semester in December 20XX, can also be broken into steps:

- **Step 1:** Review registration process and tuition cost online
- **Step 2:** Begin saving enough for admissions fee and first two classes
- **Step 3:** Complete application
- **Step 4:** Have transcripts forwarded to the Admissions Office
- **Step 5:** Meet with Admissions Counselor to determine what courses are transferrable and what's still needed
- **Step 6:** Register for first two courses
- **Step 7:** Buy books for first two courses
- **Step 8:** Prepare for and attend first semester
- **Step 9:** Study enough to achieve no lower than a C on any course
- **Step 10:** Save, register, buy books, attend, and pass two courses per semester
- **Step 11:** Graduate December 20XX

Breaking the effort down into steps helps keep any long-term goal in perspective, particularly once you realize you don't have to do anything other than take the next step and then you're one step closer to your goal.

**Relevant:** The relevance of any goal is the *WHY*. If this goal isn't important enough for you to carve out enough time to nurture it and move it toward fruition, why would you choose this particular goal?

When I first started in the food service industry all I wanted to do was be a bartender. The bartenders where I worked were so cool and all of the attractive patrons flocked to them. The first ten years I was a bartender I seriously worked at it. I developed a persona and a following that insured no matter where I worked, my regulars followed me.

I even managed bars a half dozen times, but typically burned out after about a year working for owners who were more than willing to have me work 100-hour weeks until I couldn't think straight.

I watched every single episode of Bar Rescue and could walk into a bar and within an hour know the top three things that needed to change to take it to the next level. I loved this business; however, I finally concluded that I wouldn't be satisfied until I completed my next chapter.

Finding my next chapter was the problem. It wasn't until I realized that my real longing was to figure out how to get my whole family living in the same geographical area was what I really wanted. When I stood on that beach on Amelia Island I knew this was the place.

I wasn't certain how to make it happen but I knew it was where I wanted to be and that my family all wanted to be there too. I'd like to say it was all smooth sailing after that; however, we're still working through the details.

I made the move but hurt myself badly in the process. With two broken fingers and a hand that needed a least a month of recovery time my Plan A: move down to Amelia Island, find a bartending job, hone my handyman skills, and open a small business as a handyman had to be placed on hold.

I had to do something but I wasn't certain what it was. I was driven. My entrepreneurial spirit went into overdrive. I could hardly sleep thinking and planning the next ten projects I could do. The hardest thing was to focus on what I could do that would pave the way to help me reach my next chapter.

That's when I realized my next chapter was writing the book I'd always wished I'd read – the one you're reading today.

If you're not spending every extra minute you can carve out pursuing your goal, ask yourself:

- Why am I pursuing <u>this</u> goal?
- Why is it important to me?
- Can I close my eyes and see what achieving this goal looks like?
- Am I doing this for me or to meet someone else's expectations?

**Time-Based:** With your specific, measurable, achievable, and relevant goal defined, you can now develop the plan to get there. Using the steps you defined to convince yourself your goal is achievable you assign a date to each step. Making the goal for writing this book became:

- **Step 1:** Complete first draft of the book by Feb 16, 20XX.
- **Step 2:** Upload manuscript and complete cover by Feb 17, 20XX.
- **Step 3:** Get format approval and order proof from fulfillment provider by Feb 20, 20XX
- **Step 4:** Join Chamber of Commerce by March 16, 20XX
- **Step 5:** Develop a Marketing Plan by March 18, 20XX
- **Step 6:** Register publishing business and obtain tax ID by March 18, 20XX
- **Step 7:** Open business bank account by March 18, 20XX
- **Step 8:** Get charge machine by March 23, 20XX
- **Step 9:** Edit and upload changes to the proof by Feb 28,

20XX
- **Step 10:** Publish the book by March 16, 20XX
- **Step 11:** Order and receive copies by March 23, 20XX
- **Step 12:** Publicize the book by March 31, 20XX
- **Step 13:** Begin sales by March 31, 20XX

Establishing the end date for meeting the other goal I've been using as an example, that of earning an Associate's Degree in Liberal Arts from Jacksonville Community College by the winter semester in December 20XX, can't be established until Step 5 is reached. This is because you finally get the information you need to be able to establish the end date. That shouldn't stop you from establishing the dates for Steps 1-5. Once you complete Step 5 it's important to set those dates:

**Step 1:** Review registration process and tuition cost online by June 1, 20XX.

**Step 2:** Save enough for admissions fee and first two classes by November 15, 20XX

**Step 3:** Complete application by November 15, 20XX

**Step 4:** Have transcripts forwarded to the Admissions Office by November 15, 20XX

**Step 5:** Meet with Admissions Counselor to determine what courses are transferrable and what's still needed by December 7, 20XX.

**Step 6:** Set date to reach Step 11 and register for first two courses

**Step 7:** Buy books for first two courses

**Step 8:** Prepare for and attend first semester

**Step 9:** Study enough to achieve no lower than a C on any course

**Step 10:** Save, register, buy books, attend, and pass two courses per semester

**Step 11:** Graduate December 20XX

**EXECUTING YOUR PLAN:** Now that your goal is a smart one because it's specific, measurable, achievable, relevant and time-based, it can be succinctly stated. In the first example it can be stated as: "My book to help other bartenders be financially successful will be ready for sale by April 1$^{st}$, 20XX.

It's important at this point to focus on Step 1. If you get caught up in how you're going to achieve every single step you'll spend all your time figuring that out and never getting started.

This happened to me when I was writing this book. I got so overwhelmed with the enormity of the effort and had so many other things going on in my life that it was difficult to focus for even an hour a day on getting anything done on the book. I could find a million and one excuses not to just sit down and write. I finally figured out I needed to carve out a certain amount of time each day to work on it. Once I understood that even spending an hour a day working toward a goal I wanted to achieve would help move me down the path, I was able to quiet my mind enough to focus.

Once your smart goal is defined, write it out and place it where you'll see it at the beginning and the end of each day.  Now review it and recommit to it at the beginning of each day.  At the end of each day review it again and make a commitment to yourself regarding what you're going to do to reach it the next day.

Sometimes you'll miss a date you set for a step.  When that happens, review your goal and make certain you're committed to reaching it.  If so, reset the dates and get going.  If not, why not?  Was it really something you wanted to do?  What got in the way?

Facing these questions can and will be difficult.  It's hard to face our deficiencies and mistakes.  But you're strong enough and you're worth the effort.  We owe it to ourselves and our loved ones to work to become the best versions of ourselves we can be.

By becoming financially successful you can finally take the time to give your loved ones your attention, your full attention, instead of always worrying that you need to rush off to another job or another shift.

They deserve that from you and you deserve the opportunity to fully enjoy them and to be present in your own life.  You're worth it.

## Step 10: Getting Started

One of the pivotal points of my life (so far) was the day I realized how miserable one of my financially successful regulars was. Even though he'd achieved what he'd set out to do financially, had dozens of friends, and had time to do anything he wanted to do, he typically didn't leave the bar each day until he'd been cut off. From what he said, I gathered he'd go home, turn on the television and pass out. The next day he'd be back at the bar doing the same thing.

Then it hit me … the trajectory of my life was on the same path as his – except for the financially successful part. I'd work a shift, have some drinks, go home, turn on a comedy program, pass out for a few hours, then get up and do the same thing the next day.

I kept everyone at arm's length. I'd sabotaged countless romantic relationships when things got too close. I was so tired of being everyone's best friend, confidante, and favorite bartender that when I had a few hours off, I was only hoping for some quiet time. I had a million friends, but I was incapable of truly caring for any of them.

My health was abysmal. At least a couple of times a week I'd barely be able to get out of bed. My stomach hurt all the time and I always seemed to be recovering from or trying to recover from a cold.

I'd make list after list of things I needed to do, look at them and be so overwhelmed I'd have trouble getting started.

Then my family had a crisis. One of those shake you to your core, what the heck is really important, crises. I had to step up and get real.

While I was doing the things I needed to do for them I realized, with a blinding flash of the obvious, that it was essential for me to take care of my own business as well or, instead of helping my family, I would be contributing to the problem. My every-day financial success was doing nothing other than bridging the gap over the chasm of positively contributing to my family's well-being.

**POSITIVE AFFIRMATIONS:** Part of the problem was my internal dialogue. Although the jury is still out on how many thoughts each of us have a day, with credible studies that cite the number from 10,000 to 60,000, even if the number is on the low end – it's no wonder we're exhausted.

For most of us, these thoughts are often more negative than positive, particularly when our actions are incongruent with our thinking. This was the case for me. Every good thing I wanted to experience was directly related to fifty things I hadn't done. I was living a very fun, entirely worthless life and hadn't yet confronted why I was willing to work 114-hour weeks to avoid addressing the things that would allow me to relax and feel as if I had accomplished something. On reflection, if one of my friends ever talked to me the way I used to talk to myself, he wouldn't have been my friend for very long.

One day I was particularly frustrated with myself. I'd finally dragged myself out of bed and was standing in front of the mirror brushing my teeth when I really looked at myself. Staring back at me was the same look of tiredness and defeat I was feeling. My eyes hadn't looked rested in twelve years of bar pictures.

I decided right then and there that no one could help me get out of the rut I was in except me. I finished brushing my teeth, looked at myself again and said out loud, "No one can change your situation but you and you can do better than this. You're strong enough to face every challenge and you're worth fighting for."

Strangely enough I immediately felt a little better. Not "woo woo" better, but clearer and stronger.

I talked to my bestie later that day and told her about the experience.

She smiled knowingly and shared with me that what I'd experienced was the power of a positive affirmation.

Since then, when I'm doing something that requires me to stand in front of the mirror, I've paused, given myself a smile, and said something positive. These ten seconds improve my entire day, my outlook on the day, and my ability to enjoy every single day.

**THE TED TALK:** One of the things I believed about myself was that I was a procrastinator and there were people in my life who were important to me that actually said that about me to me. No holds barred.

Then I watched a hilarious Ted Talk about procrastination by Tim Urban, a blogger whose *'Wait but Why'* explores procrastination. He described his early theory that procrastinator's brains were different than non-procrastinators. You can check it out at: https://www.ted.com/talks/tim_urban_inside_the_mind_of_a_master_procrastinator

He tested this theory by arranging MRIs of his brain and a friend's who he believed was not a procrastinator. He described the results in his TED Talk; illustrated with pictures that looked to have been drawn by a fourth grader. Both brains had a Rational Decision Maker who is depicted with a steering wheel one would see on a ship; however, the procrastinator's brain also has an Instant Gratification

Monkey. Every time a procrastinator starts to do something that's necessary to keep his ship on course, the Instant Gratification Monkey takes over, grabs the steering wheel and replaces it with an activity that was fun and completely non-productive, but quickly produces a visible result.

When a deadline approaches, the third character living in the procrastinator's brain, the Panic Monster, takes over and scares the Instant Gratification Monkey back up into his tree so the Rational Decision Maker can take over long enough for the activity to be completed, typically at an irrational pace.

Tim Urban went on to explain that after the TED talk, he received thousands of EMAILs from people saying they had the same problem and how frustrated they were that they couldn't control the Monkey. EMAILS came from doctors, engineers, lots of PhD students; people who had great accomplishments they felt nothing about. Seeing this made him realize there are two types of things we procrastinate about: those that have deadlines and those that don't, **but we're all procrastinating about something!**

We all have a Rational Decision Maker, an Instant Gratification Monkey, and a Panic Monster in one form or another. The problem is, unfortunately, activities that have no deadline don't wake up our Panic Monster. So, any endeavor that involves some effort to get started doesn't wake up the Panic Monster, because there is no deadline. Activities such as: taking care of your health, exercising, or tending to your relationships, can go undone.

In other words, the activities that, when neglected, cause us no end of regrets, grief and unhappiness can make us feel like spectators in our own lives.

He ended his TED talk with a graphic showing a life calendar comprised of a box for each week of a ninety-year old life. He observed that we've all used up some of our boxes and maybe we each need to take a hard look at what we are procrastinating about.

The realization that everyone is procrastinating about something made me realize I'm no different than anyone else and we all share this issue.

This understanding empowered me to confront that I could choose to quit letting myself be overwhelmed with everything I had to do and get on with it.

**GETTING OUT OF YOUR OWN WAY:** With this knowledge, it occurred to me that if everyone is procrastinating about something, everyone probably has something about themselves that's getting in the way of their success or happiness. (And some of us have more than one thing!)

**Addictions** are probably at the top of the list. If your dependence on alcohol, drugs, cigarettes, sex, social media, or Snickers is getting in the way of your financial success, your relationships, or what you want to do with your life, facing up to it would be a relief. It would be a tough thing to confront, but perhaps the juice would be worth the squeeze.

Even if there are no side effects yet but you know what you're doing will have long term implications and perhaps this is the time to address the issue.

Addictions behave just like the Instant Gratification Monkey from the Ted Talk. Like any change, there's a simple process we can follow to make and positively approach that change.

- **Activity 1: Make the Decision**. Depending upon your addiction and the effect it's having on your life, you'll need to decide if you need help to quit, can quit cold turkey, or just need to get it under control. If you decide to get help, do it. If you decide to quit cold turkey, do it. If you decide to control it, which is often where many of us start, then here's a process to determine if you have the where-with-all to do just that.

Imagine how different your life will be without the monkey being in the way of what you're trying to accomplish. I've found that once I acknowledge to myself that my reason for change is more important to me than the addiction that's getting in the way of my happiness, I have a compelling reason to stick with beating the monkey. Honestly, it's hard to gain traction with the weight of that monkey on your back.

It is empowering to develop a positive affirmation that you can use to start each day. For example: "I am in charge of how much I drink. I can stay sober long enough to get what I need done completed today." Say this positive affirmation every morning when you get up and call it into mind any time the Instant Gratification Monkey wants to take over.

- **Activity 2: Establish Your Baseline.** If you're going to get the monkey under control, it's important to keep score so you know who's winning. Using the journal we talked about in Step 3 to track your earning/spending and "to do" list, pick a section to record when you fed the monkey (drank, smoked, etc.), where you were, and why you fed your old habits.

At the end of the week during your business meeting, take a look at your journal and analyze what your patterns were.

First, count the total for each day and figure out the difference between what was going on during the days you fed the monkey the most and those you fed him the least. You might find that you feed him more on days when you pull a double or on your days off. It's easier to feed him when you're so worn out or stressed that you're seeing double, even when your eyes are closed.

Next, analyze the trigger. The analysis might show you, "I always have drinks after work" or "I always have a cigarette before I take a shower". There's always a recognizable trigger once you become aware of your pattern.

- **Activity 3: Begin to Cage the Monkey.** Now that you are beginning to understand your triggers, use the lowest number for each type of day as your baseline. For the next two weeks make the commitment that you won't go over that number. Hell, for the next two hours, commit to it; you've worked crazy-ass shifts where two hours pass in a blink, you can do this easily.

Record your progress in your journal. If you let the monkey out of the cage for a day, take a minute and understand why. Don't make excuses, just review what happened, repeat your affirmation, and start again the next day.

- **Activity 4: Begin to Tame the Monkey.** Once you've successfully caged him, you can start to tame him by slowly limiting the amount and window of time when he's allowed to play. Choose to either reduce the amount of your consumption or the times when you consume. For example, if you were smoking 30 cigarettes a day, reduce it by one to 29 a day; if you were having your first drink when you got up, wait an hour. (I found that if I got busy doing something on my list, that hour would fly by AND I'd get something done. Not a bad trade-off.)

Over time, you'll figure out whether this is an addiction that you can control or not. If you're making progress in the right direction, yet slipping up sometimes, just keep at it.

If you see no progress, it might be time to admit you can't do it on your own. There's no shame in that. Just find the type of help that will work for you. Some of the coolest people and bartenders I've ever had the pleasure of slinging with had been to court-issued AA. Seems that it takes more strength to confront an issue than it does to fight it.

**Treat Yourself Better:** The next category of behaviors where we get in our own way are the ones associated with the choices we make or fail to make.

- **Activity 1: Get Good Sleep**. Unless you're one of the lucky few with set shifts that are the same every day and those shifts match up with the hours of places you need to go and the people you need to see, getting enough sleep requires attention.

I don't know about you, but when I haven't had enough sleep nothing is any fun, everything irritates me, and I feel like I'm phoning it in. I found that just a few changes in my personal habits help ensure the time when I can sleep that I actively relax enough to sleep.

**Step 1: Establish A Quiet Time:** Be certain to let your friends and family know when your quiet time is. Trust me when I tell you, they'll be thrilled to know you're not going to be answering their calls before 2 PM because you're sleeping. I was blown away when I finally told my mom that her 10 AM phone calls were waking me up and she said, "I didn't realize that. What's a better time to call?" She was as tired of talking to Grumpy Tony as I was at getting called in the "morning".

Now she never calls before 2 PM. Our relationship is stronger and more beneficial than ever because we know and respect each other's boundaries.

Once you establish a quiet time, even if you can't sleep, use the time for yourself. Read a book, watch a movie, play with your cat, but unplug. You're worth 20 minutes to spend on yourself, right?

**Step 2: Establish a Sleep Routine:** Our minds are wired to recognize patterns of behavior. They recognize "put on my sleep clothes, take out my contacts, wash my face, brush my teeth" as what we do when we get ready to sleep.

**Step 3: Establish a Pleasant Sleep Place:** The place you

sleep should be personalized to what helps you relax (have you ever noticed that sometimes when you have an overnight guest or sleep somewhere else you're still tired when you get up?). If clutter irritates you, declutter. Give yourself the gift of clean sheets and a clean pillow. The quality of your sleep will determine how tomorrow goes and how you approach it.

- **Activity 2: Eat and Drink Wisely.** Just face it. Most of what we eat is bar food. It's breaded, deep fried, covered in cheese, or has loads of sodium, calories, and very few nutrients. In other words, we eat like we're still five years old.

It's also convenient, we get a discount, and we don't have to cook it ourselves. Other than the fact we're probably exhausted all the time because we're not getting the nutrients our body needs and setting ourselves up for a miserable old age of medical complaints, why would we attempt to do better?

Changing that behavior isn't going to happen overnight, but wouldn't it be great to start feeding your body what it needs to be happy? You can start to change it and very quickly you'll start to see quantifiable benefits.

**Step 1: Learn to Cook One Healthy Meal.** In case no one ever mentioned it, being able to cook for yourself or wow the hottie you're trying to impress with a healthy and delicious meal is worth the effort. Even if it's only a pre-cooked chicken, a salad, and a side, you'll feel better after you've made it, and your date will be impressed.

Add one healthy meal to your repertoire every month. They don't have to be complicated.

**Step 2: Learn to Eat Green Food.** When I was five my kindergarten class listened to a presentation on food safety. At dinner that night I looked solemnly at the spinach on my plate and announced to my family, "I don't eat green food." I stuck to that for years and wouldn't even eat green Jell-O.

Fresh vegetables are one of the nicest things we can do to make our bodies healthy. You might start with only one a week, but figuring out how to get one into a meal every day is worth it.

One of the benefits of most green foods is they help keep us "regular" and that alone is worth incorporating them into our diet. This definitely limits the stomach aches by the middle of an eight- or twelve-hour shift.

- **Activity 3: Check in with your Doc**. Partner with your primary care doctor so he or she can help you stay well instead of just treating you when you're sick. We're all a little bit different and when there's a change in your lab values, it may not be noticed if you don't go in for a check-up once a year while you're well enough to establish your norms.

By building a regular relationship with your primary care doctor, when you're sick she can tell what's changed in your body chemistry that might be causing any problem you might have. The doctor might find a change in your body chemistry early on that otherwise wouldn't have been noticed.

If you only ever see a doctor at an acute care clinic or, worse yet, emergency room, they're treating the illness rather than working to keep you well. They're helping treat the symptoms instead of helping you identify and combat the cause.

- **Activity 4: Save Your Smile.** Did you know that one of the methods of assessing the health of an animal is their dental health? Human animals are no different. In fact, the US Armed Forces won't deploy a service member to a combat zone who has dental issues.

Yet many of us don't visit the dentist regularly. A little cavity caught at six months can easily be fixed. By the time it starts to bother you it's often already touching a nerve and requires invasive care that can weaken the structure of the tooth.

A professional dental cleaning every six months keeps plaque and bacteria from homesteading in your mouth. This helps to prevent not only cavities but gum disease.

The kicker here is preventive dental care is typically covered by dental insurance policies that cost about $30 a month, whereas remedial dental care is never fully covered and can cost the price of a new car. Another preventive measure is to leave the sugary caffeine drinks that permeate your dental enamel in the convenience store or bar cooler. They are an insidious threat to your dental health and they're ridiculously expensive. Are caffeine, guanine and taurine worth $4.95 for 8 ounces and an hour of feeling decent before you crash and fall? Hmm....

Who in their right mind thinks having their teeth sit in a cleaning mixture by their sink every night is sexy?

- **Activity 5: Manage Your Stress.** It's obvious that life today is more stressful than ever before. I attribute this to the constant barrage of information coming our way. We have so many stimuli shoved in our faces all the time, it's acutely uncomfortable when we try to disconnect and give ourselves a little attention and time to relax, settle, and reset.

It's essential to develop the willingness and ability to be able to quiet your mind. Years ago, a mentor recommended <u>The Four Agreements</u>, by Don Miguel Ruiz. The book offers readers four agreements you can make with yourself that, if followed, have a profound effect upon how you live your life and the effect other people have on you. The book changed my life.

**The first of these agreements, "Be Impeccable with Your Word"** is so basic and rudimentary one would expect it to be one of the baseline tenets of our lives. As with any lesson, the approach you take to applying it to your life is based upon what it means to you.

Being impeccable with your word takes many forms and has many implications:

➢ **Telling the truth:** We each know when we're telling the truth and when we're stretching it. Whether I'm representing myself or the business I'm working for, there should be only one version of the truth as I see it. It involves acknowledging that what I understand to be true might not be someone else's truth and that it's wise to be open to understanding their perspective.

➢ **Keeping commitments:** This is something that's so essential to improving the probability you'll be successful and it's easy to start addressing and being true to. Only make commitments you believe you can meet. Once you've made a commitment, do everything within your power to meet it, whether it's to a client or a colleague. If you find that for some reason you can't meet it, be honest with the person to whom you made the commitment and tell them when they can expect the promised results.

➢ **Doing a fair day's work:** When you are working, put in the required and expected effort. Don't waste time.

➢ **Producing the service your customers expect:** Don't take short cuts on the quality of your service. It represents who you are.

No one wants to work with someone they can't trust. Be impeccable with your word and people will come to trust you because they know they can depend upon you to be honest regardless of the cost.

**The second agreement is "Do Your Best Everyday".** Making and following this agreement is the best method I know to rid yourself of the guilt that comes with any type of failure. We can all recall circumstances in our lives when we didn't do our best. Either we were tired, overwhelmed, or just didn't have the energy to make the effort to show up and do our best.

Like anything else, doing your best requires practice. You can focus on these simple steps:

➢ **Managing your time:** Mindlessly surfing the web, gossiping with a co-worker, complaining about "them", whoever "they" may be, checking social media, or texting your friends: these all take time away from the time you're available to make a difference. Go in with a plan for what you're going to accomplish each day and do those things first.

➢ **Doing one thing at a time:** Multi-tasking assures that every single thing you do takes longer. Even with large, multi-day or week efforts, decide where a logical cut-off point is between finishing one activity and working on another, then work to that point before moving on to something else.

➢ **Doing quality work:** This doesn't mean perfection, but it does mean producing a product that meets the requirements for which it was intended. You should be proud of anything you produce; making sure it's quality takes as much effort as phoning it in.

Doing your best everyday means just that – with what I know and what I have to offer, this is the best I can do. I can take pride in the effort I gave, whether the result was a success or not.

**The third agreement, "If You Have a Question, ask"** prevents misperceptions from becoming disagreements. When I read this the first time it brought to mind how many times I'd sensed someone had slighted or wronged me in some way and blew it out of proportion instead of simply asking the person if he meant for me to perceive it that way.

Typically, the person either meant no harm or hadn't considered the implications from my perspective. For example, the weekly schedule comes out and your money shifts are gone. If your boss values your contribution, he probably didn't intend the switch so it's important that you ask him about it. If he did intend it, wouldn't you want to know that so you can either make a performance correction or start looking for another job?

**The fourth agreement, "Nothing Anyone Else Does is About You"** was the agreement that had the most profound effect on me. I read it several times before it started to sink in. If nothing anyone else did was about me, what in the world was I thinking when I tried to guilt other people into action or make excuses for my own issues by walking around with a 'V' on my forehead. (The 'V', of course, stands for VICTIM.)

I spent a lot of time thinking:

"If only she would do this, or he would stop doing that, my business would be a success."

"If only this would happen or that hadn't happened, I would have won that bid."

Then there was the ominous "they".

"They" stood in the way of my success.

"They" could afford to undercut my bid or put more people on any job.

After internalizing this, I realized I was wasting the energy I needed to be successful by worrying about the effect other people were having on me rather than focusing on what I needed to do to make my business successful.

By following this agreement, I finally started to get out of my own way.

**THE CHALLENGE:** If you've read this far, first of all, thank you. Second, go back to Step 1 and make the decision to take charge of not only your financial success, but your life.

No one can do it for you – thank goodness. If they could you'd either be twelve years old or it wouldn't be your life.

You CAN be financially successful AND lead a balanced life that's rich and happy.

Take care of you. You're worth it. Even without having met most of you whose eyes have perused these pages, I know and promise you: you're worth it. You got this.

Thank you for reading, thank you for giving yourself and your future some consideration, and thank you for taking a moment to consider how you can better your financial (and LIFE) situation.

Have a good night and we'll see you soon! 😊

# ACKNOWLEDGEMENTS

With all the gratitude in the world, I'd like to first thank my mother, co-author, and inspiration, Leah Ward-Lee.  Mama, you're the perfect example of how to live a successful life filled with joy, passion, and peace.

Dad and Lisa for their patience, love, and lessons.  Thank you for letting me talk my thoughts into order, for being my rocks in the mental storm, and for
teaching me that a goal is a temporary stop, not an end point.

Tina Atkinson, thank you for supporting me and being the best bestie a man could hope for.

A tremendous thank you to John and Carole for facilitating my move to paradise and getting me set up to live comfortably.

Ashleah, Willie, Jason, P-Mac, Melody, Kimberly, Malcolm, Faye, and Ciera, Michael (and the Team), and my man Bacon, thank y'all for going to war with me and propping me up during those 19-hour days and filling them with laughs.

Nina, thank you for being a bright light and beautiful spirit.

Don, Jeremy, Greg, Christian, Omar, DeShon, Carol, Royce, Brandi, David, Cary, Calvin, Delanie, Stephen, Anthony, I appreciate you showing me how to operate a successful business with passion, patience, and in the right way.

Chris and Cammi, Bender and Karalie, Delanie, Stephen, Anthony, Heather, Alexa, Neely, Mac, Aimi, TC, Alexander, Marcus, Patrick, Marte, Amanda, Alex, Abby, Jeff, Gary, David, Joe, Dale, Jerrod, Angela, JC, and Jeni, thank you guys for Everything.  Your friendship and love have made me a better man and an even luckier friend.

Tysun, thank you for battling with me and showing me that pride, drive, and care for your craft will always get you through.

And to the hundreds of teammates and thousands of regulars I've enjoyed through the years, all my love and appreciation.

You're why I do what I do.  I love you.

# ABOUT THE AUTHORS

## Tony X. Lee

Tony Lee has spent a lifetime in the bar and restaurant business since restocking a napkin holder at a CiCi's Pizza when he was fifteen years old. There have been brief forays into managing a shoe store and writing music, but for twenty years, slinging drinks, running successful concepts, and training passionate staff members has been his joy, focus, and livelihood.

He decided to write this book after breaking a couple of fingers forced him to consider what we do well, what we lack, and how easy it could be for all of us to relax, be comfortable, and enjoy the fruits of our labor. He currently resides a two-minute walk from the ocean on Amelia Island with his 24-pound bag of love, the Kitty Princess Mylo.

## Leah Ward-Lee

Author's Photo by: Gerry Burns, www.GerryBurns.com

Leah Ward-Lee is a serial micro-entrepreneur. She opened her first business at ten after lobbying for and receiving a shoe shine kit for Christmas. She pulled her wagon through the neighborhood, going door-to-door, offering to shine her neighbor's shoes for twenty-five cents a pair. Once her wagon was full, she took the shoes home and polished them.

Unfortunately, that business was short-lived. She hadn't tagged the shoes and couldn't remember whose shoes were whose, so her dad went with her to retrace the route until every pair was returned.

Since then she's had businesses developing and teaching college courses, instructing aerobic classes, owning half a plane that was rented to a flight and maintenance school, and renting homes. She's also owned a consignment store, a gift shop, a gift basket business, a consulting firm, hosted *The Executive Toolbox* (a weekly radio show), and a publishing company.

She lived twenty years in the US Army, served as the Chief Information and Technical Officer for two major insurance companies, and has a second career as a management consultant.

Leah resides in Dallas, TX, and on Amelia Island with Sammy and Goliath, her two rescue dogs.

Follow Leah at *www.1000dollarstartups.com*

www.ingramcontent.com/pod-product-compliance
Lightning Source LLC
LaVergne TN
LVHW051846080426
835512LV00018B/3092